Not Who We Are

Don't Call Yourself What the Curse Has Called You!

Aaron Maxwell Montague

NOT WHO WE ARE
Don't Call Yourself What the Curse Has Called You!

Published by:

Kingdom Publishing
1350 Blair Drive, Suite F
Odenton, MD 21113

Printed in the United States of America

ISBN: 978-1-967006-11-3 (Paperback)
ISBN: 978-1-967006-12-0 (Ebook)

Dedication

To my beloved wife, Wanda B. Montague—

You are my rock, my encourager, my quiet wind of wisdom and grace.

You bring beauty where there was striving, and peace where there was pressure.

Your kindness has been my language of love, your laughter my restoration, your faith my reminder that God's promises are still yes and amen.

Through long nights and rewrites, you have stood beside me—not only as the love of my life, but as the living embodiment of patience and support.

You believed in this work when it was only a whisper, and your belief made it a song.

I love you eternally.

Thank you, Sweetheart—for every prayer, every smile, and every moment of steadfast love.

Acknowledgments

First and always, I give glory to God, the Author and Finisher of my faith—the One who spoke light into darkness and identity into confusion. Every revelation, every page, every pause in this work belongs to Him.

To my beloved wife, Wanda "God-Is-Love" Montague, whose presence makes every house a home. Your encouragement, wisdom, and quiet strength have steadied me more times than I can count.

You are the melody of kindness in my life, the soft answer that turns away wrath, the grace that keeps me grounded in love.

To my children, Aaron Arnesto and Valerie, and to my grandchildren, Max and Sam—you are the living proof that God's promises travel through generations. May every word of this book remind you of your divine identity and call you to walk in truth, boldness, and compassion.

To my mother, Jeannie Montague, whose prayers still cover me, and in loving memory of my father, Horace Montague, whose work ethic and integrity taught me what perseverance looks like. Your legacy breathes through every syllable of my purpose.

To my extended family—brothers, sisters, cousins, friends— thank you for reminding me that love is thicker than blood when it is rooted in faith, laughter, and forgiveness.

To my spiritual family at Kingdom Celebration Center and to Apostle Dr. Antonio and Pastor Dr. Barbara Palmer, thank you for your trust, covering, and example of servant leadership. Your ministries have modeled what kingdom collaboration truly means.

To every teacher, scholar, pastor, coach, and mentor who poured wisdom into me when I was still finding my voice—I honor your seeds. They have taken root here.

And finally, to the African diaspora—scattered, scarred, yet still standing—this book is for you. May it remind us all that our names were never meant to be curses, but covenants of greatness.

Table of Contents

Foreword

There are books that inform, books that inspire, and then there are books that awaken. *Not Who We Are* belongs in the latter category. It is more than words on a page—it is a trumpet blast against silence, a prophetic summons to remember who we truly are in the eyes of God.

Aaron Maxwell Montague has written with both the mind of a scholar and the heart of a prophet. He lays bare the reality that words are never neutral; they are spiritual instruments that shape destinies. For centuries, language has been wielded as a weapon of oppression, forging chains not only upon bodies but upon minds, souls, and generations. In these pages, Montague unmasks the curse embedded in words like *Negro, Nigger,* and *Nigga,* tracing their origins and exposing the hidden spiritual contracts they represent.

Yet this book is not one of despair—it is a declaration of deliverance. Montague points us back to the divine pattern of Scripture, Torah, and Qur'an, where names are never incidental but covenantal. Abram became Abraham. Jacob became Israel. Simon became Peter. Each renaming was not cosmetic but transformative, marking a shift in destiny. Likewise, he calls a generation to renounce cursed identities and reclaim the names that Heaven has spoken over them.

What you hold in your hands is both history and prophecy. It is history, because it courageously uncovers the deliberate design of linguistic bondage and its devastating psychological, cultural, and spiritual effects. It is prophecy, because it calls forth a future where communities rise, speak truth, and silence the echoes of oppression with the language of blessing.

This book will make you think deeply. It will stir your emotions. At times, it will confront you with hard truths about the words we have normalized and the identities we have unconsciously accepted.

But if you receive its message, it will also empower you with a fresh vocabulary of life, dignity, and destiny.

I commend this work to every pastor, teacher, parent, leader, and seeker of truth. Read it prayerfully. Reflect on its questions. Speak its declarations aloud. And above all, let it remind you: you are not what the curse has called you. You are who God has named you to be.

May this book awaken a generation to rise from linguistic ashes into the fullness of their God-given identity.

— Bishop Dr. Antonio M. Palmer, D.Div
Kingdom Alliance of Churches International

Preface / Author's Note

There comes a moment in every generation when truth refuses to stay silent—when the Spirit of God begins to stir in the souls of the misnamed and the misunderstood. That moment is now.

This message burned in my bones long before it became a manuscript. I can still hear my father's voice, firm and loving, warning me: "Don't you ever let anybody call you that word." But I can also hear the echo of the streets, the laughter of the broken, the normalization of a curse repeated in ignorance—spoken by us, about us, as if the chains had been rebranded as culture.

This book was born out of that tension: the holy war between who God says we are and what the curse has tried to name us. Not Who We Are is both revelation and revolution. It's a trumpet blast across centuries of silence. It is the sound of a people rising, shaking off linguistic ashes, and stepping into prophetic identity.

Words are not harmless. They are spiritual vehicles. They create atmospheres. They open doors or close them. From the Torah to the Qur'an to the Gospel, God shows us that names are destinies spoken aloud. When heaven names you, blessing follows. When hell names you, bondage begins.

But I came to tell you—our mouths are powerful enough to break every agreement made in ignorance! The same tongue that cursed can bless. The same voice that answered to falsehood can call forth truth. The same generation that repeated the slur can now prophesy its extinction.

This is not a book to read; it's a declaration to release. Every page is a call to wake up, speak up, and rise up. For we are not what they called us.

We are what God has called us to be.

— Aaron Maxwell Montague

Part 1

THE CURSE

Chapter 1
The Tongue as a Weapon and a Wand

"Death and life are in the power of the tongue: and they that love it shall eat the fruit thereof."
— Proverbs 18:21

"Have you not seen how Allah sets forth a parable of a good word being like a good tree—firmly rooted and its branches reaching to the sky?"
— Qur'an, Surah Ibrahim 14:24

"I call heaven and earth to record this day against you, that I have set before you life and death, blessing and cursing: therefore choose life..."
— Deuteronomy 30:19

A Name I Could Never Escape

From as early as I can remember, one thing was made crystal clear in my home and in my community:

Don't let anyone call you "nigger."

It was taught with solemnity, reinforced with passion, and echoed from generation to generation. This word was off-limits — a violent, denigrating word, forged in the furnace of hate. If someone used it against you, you were to stand up, speak out, and never accept it.

And yet... in the very same breath, I heard it everywhere.

In the neighborhood. On the porch. At the basketball court. In the barbershop. At family cookouts.

Adults used it. Teens used it. It was spoken as greeting and insult, as joke and nickname, as casual punctuation.

"Nigga, pass the ball!"

1

"Nigga, you crazy!"

"That's my nigga!"

The word that was forbidden from outsiders was normalized among ourselves. It was a local colloquialism. It floated through conversations like a rhythm we had all learned to tap our feet to—without fully realizing the music's origin.

Then came the moment that branded itself into my memory.

The Day My Father Drew the Line

I was still a boy when it happened. A white friend of mine, meaning no harm, used the word around me. Not in a hateful way—not with a sneer or a slur—but in the same casual, rhythmic tone he'd heard from us. He was imitating, not attacking.

But when my father heard it, his face turned to steel.

He pulled me aside with that unmistakable father's gravity.

"Son," he said, "Don't you ever let anybody call you that. I don't care if they're white, Black, or anything else. Don't you ever let that word come out of their mouth about you. That's not your name."

There was power in his voice—ancestral power. It was as if my father was standing not just as a parent, but as a guardian of identity, drawing a spiritual boundary line in the sand.

And I felt it deep in my soul.

But even then, part of me wrestled. Why was this word treated like a curse from one direction, and like a nickname from another? How could a single word be both forbidden and familiar, despised and embraced, external poison and internal slang?

Words Are More Than Sounds — They're Spiritual Instruments

The answer didn't fully unfold until years later, when I began to understand the spiritual technology of language.

God didn't use a hammer to make the universe. He used words.

"And God said, Let there be light: and there was light." — Genesis 1:3

The Torah, the Qur'an, and the Bible all affirm that words have creative power.

- In the Torah, God blesses and curses by speaking (Numbers 6:22–27).
- In Proverbs, life and death are in the power of the tongue (Proverbs 18:21).
- In the Qur'an, a good word is like a tree with deep roots and expansive branches (Surah Ibrahim 14:24–27).

Words don't just describe reality—they shape it. They frame identity. They build nations or break them.

This is why God repeatedly renamed people to realign them with divine destiny:

- Abram became Abraham.
- Jacob became Israel.
- Simon became Peter.
- In the Qur'an, Yahya (John) was named by God Himself (Surah Maryam 19:7).

Names call forth futures. And when the wrong name is spoken over a people, it's not just a mislabeling—it's an act of spiritual warfare.

The Enemy's Weapon: The Tongue of Oppression

The words niggard, negro, nigger, and later nigga were not just linguistic accidents. They were deliberately forged tools in the arsenal of empire, slavery, and colonialism.

They were meant to define us from the outside in, to trap us inside a narrative of inferiority, laziness, ignorance, and subhuman status. Over centuries, these words moved from foreign tongues into our own mouths, until we ourselves began to echo the curses spoken over us.

The tragedy is that what began as an external weapon became an internal rhythm.

We began to call ourselves what the curse called us.

The Fork in the Road

When I look back at that conversation with my father, I realize he was doing more than protecting me from an insult. He was standing between a curse and a covenant.

He was declaring, in his own way,

"Choose life, son." (Deut. 30:19)

He was saying: Don't agree with the enemy's dictionary.

Because every time we allow a cursed name to stick, we give that word permission to shape our destiny. But when we reject it and speak God's name over ourselves, we uproot the tree of lies and plant the tree of life.

A Word to the Reader

This book is not simply about semantics. It's about spiritual survival, historical clarity, and linguistic liberation. It's about refusing to carry into the future the verbal shackles forged in the past.

It's about answering the question God asked Adam in the Garden:

"Who told you that you were naked?" (Genesis 3:11)

And rephrasing it for our generation:

"Who told you that your name was nigger?"

Not Who We Are

Chapter 2
The Five Words That Bound a People

"My people are destroyed for lack of knowledge."
— Hosea 4:6

"Let us cut them off from being a nation; that the name of Israel may be no more in remembrance."
— Psalm 83:4

"And do not defame one another, nor call each other by [offensive] nicknames."
— Qur'an 49:11

"Out of the same mouth proceed blessing and cursing. My brethren, these things ought not so to be."
— James 3:10

Introduction: The Invisible Chains

Chains don't always clank. Some are made not of iron, but of ink, sound, and memory. Some are forged not in shipyards, but in dictionaries and classrooms. Some are passed down not by shackles on wrists, but by words on tongues.

For more than four centuries, a series of five powerful words have been spoken over the descendants of Africa. These words have framed their identities, distorted their self-concepts, and justified their subjugation. Each word carries a story — not just of language, but of power, history, and spiritual warfare.

7

These are the five:

Negroid. Negro. Niggard. Nigger. Nigga.

We must examine them like forensic investigators at the scene of a long-standing crime — because language itself has been the crime scene.

1. Negroid – The Pseudoscientific Cage

Definition & Origin:

"Negroid" emerged in 18th–19th century Europe during the rise of racial "science." European naturalists such as Johann Friedrich Blumenbach classified humanity into "Caucasoid," "Mongoloid," "Malayan," "American," and "Negroid" groups based on physical features. The suffix "-oid" means "resembling" or "like," implying not people, but types.

Function:

Negroid was never a name chosen by Africans. It was a taxonomic label meant to reduce a continent of nations into a single racial type — to flatten Yoruba, Akan, Wolof, Zulu, and countless others into one scientifically manageable category. It stripped away identity and imposed classification.

Spiritual Impact:

By calling someone "Negroid," colonial science wasn't naming them — it was caging them. It was speaking over them: "You are not a person; you are a specimen."

The Curse: Negroid was the intellectual shackle.
It was the label of dehumanization dressed up as science.

2. Negro – The Colonial Label

Definition & Origin:

"Negro" comes from the Spanish and Portuguese negro, meaning "black," from the Latin niger. European colonizers adopted this term in the 16th century to describe Africans they enslaved and trafficked to the Americas.

Function:

Negro was used in slave ledgers, colonial censuses, church rolls, and laws. It became the official racial category in the Western Hemisphere. It erased tribal, national, and cultural identity, replacing it with a color-based, colonial identity.

Spiritual Impact:

"Negro" was not a compliment. It was a way of saying: "You have no name of your own. Your identity is whatever we say your color is."

Even when it was used "politely," it carried the weight of ownership.

The Curse: Negro was the legal shackle.
It was the bureaucratic name of captivity.

3. Niggard – The Phonetic Trap

Definition & Origin:

"Niggard" comes from Old Norse nigla ("to fuss about small matters") and Middle English nigard, meaning "stingy" or "miserly." It has no historical or linguistic connection to race.

Function:

Though unrelated to "nigger" in origin, its sound made it a linguistic landmine. Over time, white supremacist culture attached moral stereotypes — stingy, lazy, ignorant — to Black people through other means. The phonetic similarity helped merge these moral insults with racial labels.

Spiritual Impact:

Niggard wasn't the root of the slur — but it fertilized the soil in which it grew. The stereotype of "shiftless and lazy" was poured onto Black identity through songs, propaganda, minstrel shows, and "science," until the word "nigger" carried moral condemnation as well as racial hatred.

The Curse: Niggard was the moral shackle.
It attached vice to identity.

4. Nigger – The Whip of the Tongue

Definition & Origin:

"Nigger" arose as a contemptuous corruption of "negro" in English, especially among enslavers and colonizers in the 17th–18th centuries. Early spellings included nigre, negar, niger. Over time, "nigger" became the standard racial slur used by whites to demean Africans and their descendants.

Function:

This word was used in slave auctions, laws, sermons, songs, lynchings, and casual conversation. It was both a weapon and a worldview — a way of marking Black people as inherently inferior, subhuman, and outside the circle of dignity.

Spiritual Impact:

"Nigger" was the word spat from the mouths of mobs as they tied ropes to trees. It was whispered in classrooms, shouted in courtrooms, and sung on plantations. It was a linguistic branding iron.

The Curse: Nigger was the violent shackle.
It was the spoken whip.

5. Nigga – The Internal Echo

Definition & Origin:

"Nigga" emerged within African American Vernacular English as a phonetic reshaping of the slur — used within the community as greeting, nickname, or marker of solidarity.

Function:

Many believed that by changing the pronunciation and embracing the word, they were neutralizing its power. But what often happened instead was internal normalization. What was once a weapon became casual — even affectionate. Yet, its root remained poisoned.

Spiritual Impact:

When a people begin to call themselves by the name their oppressors cursed them with, the curse doesn't disappear — it takes root deeper. Every repetition, even casually, keeps the spiritual rhythm alive.

The Curse: Nigga is the internal shackle.
It is the echo of the whip in our own mouths.

Conclusion: Exposing the Architecture of the Curse

These five words didn't just appear. They form a linguistic ladder of subjugation:

1. Negroid – Classify.

2. Negro – Label.

3. Niggard – Stereotype.

4. Nigger – Dehumanize.

5. Nigga – Internalize.

This is how language works in the spiritual realm. First, it defines. Then, it confines. Finally, it convinces.

But once exposed, these chains can be broken. The same tongue that accepted the curse can reject it. The same mouth that echoed bondage can declare freedom.

"God does not change the condition of a people until they change what is in themselves." — Qur'an 13:11

"Choose life, that both you and your seed may live." — Deuteronomy 30:19

Not Who We Are

Chapter 3 –
The Curse Behind the Words

"You shall not take the name of the LORD your God in vain, for the LORD will not hold him guiltless who takes His name in vain."
— Exodus 20:7

"God does not change the condition of a people until they change what is in themselves."
— Qur'an 13:11

"Death and life are in the power of the tongue."
— Proverbs 18:21

Language as a Tool of Dominion

Words have always been more than sound; they are spiritual instruments of governance. In Genesis 1, God speaks light, oceans, and creatures into being. In Deuteronomy 30:19, heaven and earth are called to witness that our words align us either with blessing or cursing.

Across the Torah, the Prophets, the Gospels, and the Qur'an, the pattern is consistent:

- Names are assignments.
- Words shape reality.
- What is spoken over a people determines what is expected of them.

When European empires began to expand, they didn't only bring weapons and ships—they brought languages, categories, and narratives. They renamed lands, reclassified peoples, and rewrote destinies with ink and tongues. The curse behind the words was not accidental; it was deliberate spiritual, cultural, and political engineering.

The Curse Is Structured, Not Spontaneous

These five words didn't evolve in isolation. They are part of a system designed to:

1. Erase Indigenous Identity – Replace Yoruba, Akan, Wolof, Igbo, etc., with "Negro."
2. Degrade Personhood – Attach moral and intellectual inferiority to Blackness.
3. Legitimize Oppression – Use language to justify slavery, colonization, and segregation.
4. Reinforce Hierarchies – Embed racism into law, religion, and science.
5. Perpetuate Through the Oppressed – Get the people themselves to internalize and repeat the curse.

Like the serpent in Eden, the curse behind these words whispered: "Who told you that you were made in God's image?" And over centuries, too many began to answer not with God's truth, but with the oppressor's vocabulary.

Historical Mechanisms of the Curse

1. Slave Codes and Legal Language

   Colonial law codified Black identity as "Negro property." People were not addressed by personal or tribal names; they were referred to generically and legally as Negroes, stripping individuality and nationhood.

2. Pseudoscience and Theology

Enlightenment racial science used "Negroid" to give a veneer of objectivity to prejudice. At the same time, twisted interpretations of scripture presented Africans as cursed descendants of Ham. These narratives legitimized "nigger" as a descriptor of inferiority.

3. Cultural Repetition

    Minstrel shows, children's books, advertisements, and music repeated these terms until they became cultural background noise. Linguistic repetition is a spiritual tactic: what is repeated often enough becomes "normal."

4. Internalization

    The final stage of the curse was to get the oppressed to use the same words on themselves. Once the community repeats the curse, the enemy doesn't have to speak it anymore.

Breaking the Curse: Returning to the Original Voice

"Who told you that you were naked?" — Genesis 3:11

God's question to Adam reverberates through the centuries. It is not merely about physical nakedness; it is about accepting a narrative that God never spoke.

To break the curse behind these words, we must:

- Recognize the structure (exposure).
- Renounce the language (repentance).
- Replace the false names with divine identity (restoration).

The Qur'an warns against defaming and using offensive nicknames (49:11). The Torah records God's repeated renaming of individuals to align them with divine destiny (Genesis 17, Numbers 6). The New Testament exhorts believers to bless and not curse (James 3). These three streams converge on one truth: God's people are not to agree with cursed names.

Conclusion: The Curse Can Be Broken

The curse behind these words is not invincible. It thrives only in ignorance and repetition. Once a generation understands the mechanism and refuses to participate, the curse collapses.

"Choose life, that both you and your seed may live." — Deuteronomy 30:19

Choosing life today means choosing different words. It means refusing to let the whip remain in our own mouths. It means declaring with clarity and courage:

"I will not call myself what the curse has called me. I will call myself what God has spoken."

Chapter 4
Psychological Warfare: Stereotypes as Chains

"For as he thinketh in his heart, so is he."
— Proverbs 23:7

"Do not defame one another, nor call each other by [offensive] nick-names. Evil is the name of wickedness after faith."
— Qur'an 49:11

"They have said, 'Come, let us cut them off from being a nation, that the name of Israel may be no more in remembrance.'"
— Psalm 83:4

Warfare Beyond the Physical

Wars are not only fought with swords, guns, and shackles. They are also fought with narratives, stereotypes, and psychological conditioning. Long after chains have been broken, laws repealed, and battlefields cleared, the residues of warfare linger in language and imagination.

For the African diaspora, the struggle against linguistic and psychological warfare has been as enduring as the fight against physical enslavement. Stereotypes have functioned as invisible shackles, binding generations through the power of repeated ideas—ideas deliberately constructed to justify subjugation.

Historical Genesis of Stereotypes

The modern racial stereotypes attached to Blackness did not arise

17

spontaneously. They were carefully engineered during the expansion of European empires. In the 17th through 19th centuries, European thinkers produced elaborate racial taxonomies, pseudoscientific "proofs," and theological justifications for slavery and colonization.

- Pseudoscientific Narratives: Figures like Johann Friedrich Blumenbach and later 19th-century anthropologists categorized Africans as "Negroid," assigning traits such as "childlike," "lazy," or "intellectually inferior." These were not observations—they were assertions crafted to fit imperial needs.
- Theological Distortions: Biblical texts were twisted to support these constructions. The "Curse of Ham" narrative, for example, was weaponized to portray Africans as divinely destined for servitude—a grave distortion not found in the Torah's own text but in colonial commentary upon it.
- Legal Codification: Colonial legal systems then embedded these stereotypes in slave codes, property laws, and social hierarchies. In many colonies, legal status hinged not on individual behavior but on racial classification—an identity tied to presumed moral and intellectual characteristics.

These stereotypes performed a dual function: they rationalized the oppression of Africans, and they ensured that even freedom would not equal full humanity in the eyes of the dominant culture.

Stereotypes as Instruments of Control

Once constructed, stereotypes became mechanisms of control more potent than physical chains. A stereotype functions like a script; once internalized by both oppressor and oppressed, it governs behavior almost automatically.

- Plantation Culture: On plantations, enslaved Africans were cast in stereotyped roles—the "happy servant," the "docile field hand," the "child needing discipline." Punishments and rewards were structured to reinforce conformity to these roles, making rebellion seem like a breach of "nature" rather than resistance to injustice.
- Post-Reconstruction Propaganda: In the United States after emancipation, films like Birth of a Nation (1915) and minstrel shows spread caricatures of ignorant, lazy, dangerous Black figures. These images justified segregation and racial violence long after slavery ended.
- Social Policy: Stereotypes informed policies that assumed Black communities were incapable of self-governance, justified unequal education funding, and shaped policing practices. The "shiftless" stereotype became a silent partner in legislation.

Unlike chains of iron, these mental chains require no jailer present. They are carried in the minds of both those who believe them and those who fear being judged by them.

Language as a Carrier of Stereotypes

Words act as vessels, carrying stereotypes across generations. A single term can compact centuries of moral judgment, racial categorization, and cultural narratives.

The infamous racial slur derived from "negro" absorbed centuries of moral stereotyping. Though linguistically unrelated to "niggard" (which means "stingy" or "miserly"), the similarity in sound facilitated a conflation of moral vice with racial identity. Over time, the slur came to embody not only racial difference but also presumed ignorance, laziness, and inferiority.

In everyday speech, jokes, and casual conversation, the repetition of such terms reinscribes the stereotype. Linguists and social psychologists note that frequent repetition of labels reinforces associative networks in the brain, making stereotypes "feel" true even when they are demonstrably false. Thus, language becomes the primary vehicle through which stereotypes travel unnoticed into new generations.

Religious and Scriptural Counter-Narratives

The Torah, the Bible, and the Qur'an consistently warn against the misuse of names and labels:

- Torah / Hebrew Bible: Names carry covenantal significance (e.g., Abram to Abraham, Jacob to Israel). Derogatory naming was often tied to foreign nations attempting to dominate Israel. Psalm 83:4 records a plot to erase the name of Israel as a nation—a linguistic and spiritual attack.
- Bible (New Testament): James 3 describes the tongue as a small member that can set the course of nature on fire. Jesus renames Simon to Peter to mark a new destiny (Matthew 16:18).
- Qur'an: Surah Al-Hujurat (49:11) explicitly prohibits mocking, defamation, and the use of offensive nicknames, declaring such behavior evil after faith has come.

Across these texts, the act of naming is never neutral; it is either an act of blessing or of cursing. Accepting derogatory names is thus more than a social choice—it is a spiritual and communal decision with long-term implications.

Modern Psychological Effects

Contemporary social psychology confirms what these scriptures have long implied: labels shape internal reality.

- Stereotype Threat: Coined by Claude Steele, this concept describes how awareness of stereotypes can impair performance. For example, when Black students are reminded of stereotypes about academic ability, their test performance often decreases—not because of actual ability, but because the stereotype creates anxiety and self-monitoring.
- Internalized Oppression: Over time, communities may begin to accept and repeat negative stereotypes about themselves. This can manifest in lowered expectations, self-limiting behaviors, or the casual use of slurs among peers.
- Linguistic Identity: Language choices affect self-perception. Studies on linguistic reclamation show mixed results: while some communities successfully neutralize former slurs, others find that continued usage keeps the stigma alive, especially when used by dominant groups.

In short, psychological warfare through language continues to influence how people see themselves and are seen by others, long after the original historical context has faded.

Conclusion: Exposing and Disarming the Chains

Stereotypes function as chains of the imagination—quiet, persistent, and difficult to detect. They were constructed through deliberate historical processes, transmitted through language, and sustained through cultural repetition.

Disarming these chains requires historical knowledge, linguistic awareness, and theological clarity. By exposing their origins, recognizing their operation in language, and countering them with divine identity and conscious speech, communities can begin to break the psychological warfare that has persisted for centuries.

This is not merely an academic exercise. It is a strategic act of liberation: to refuse the labels that were never ours, to unlearn the lies that masqueraded as heritage, and to speak over ourselves the words that align with truth, dignity, and divine purpose.

Chapter 5 – "Who Told You That Was Your Name?"

"And He said, Who told thee that thou wast naked?"
— Genesis 3:11

"For we wrestle not against flesh and blood, but against principalities, against powers, against the rulers of the darkness of this world, against spiritual wickedness in high places."
— Ephesians 6:12

"Do not defame one another, nor call each other by [offensive] nicknames. Evil is the name of wickedness after faith. And whoever does not repent, then it is those who are the wrongdoers."
— Qur'an 49:11

The Garden Question and the Invisible War

When God asked Adam, "Who told you that you were naked?" He was not merely inquiring about physical shame. He was confronting the source of a new narrative that Adam had accepted — a story that did not originate from the Creator.

In that moment, humanity faced its first identity crisis: the decision to believe a voice of deception over the voice of truth.

That question echoes through history: Who told you that you were cursed? Who told you that you were inferior? Who told you that you were anything less than what I named you to be?

The struggle over names is not just social or political. As Paul wrote in Ephesians 6:12, "We wrestle not against flesh and blood, but against principalities, against powers, against the rulers of the darkness of this world, against spiritual wickedness in high places."

23

Behind colonial labels, racial taxonomies, and slurs lies an invisible conflict — a spiritual war over identity. Labels like Negroid, Negro, and the infamous slur were not random; they were spoken into existence as curses, engineered by systems animated by spiritual wickedness to redefine a people at the level of the soul.

Names as Spiritual Covenants

Throughout the Scriptures, names are more than convenient tags. They are spiritual covenants.

- In the Torah, Abram becomes Abraham (Genesis 17), Sarai becomes Sarah, and Jacob becomes Israel (Genesis 32:28). Each renaming corresponds to a shift in destiny.
- In the Bible, Simon becomes Peter when Jesus declares, "Thou art Peter, and upon this rock I will build my church" (Matthew 16:18).
- In the Qur'an, God says, "O Zachariah, indeed We give you good tidings of a boy whose name will be Yahya. We have not assigned to any before [this] name." — Surah Maryam 19:7.

Names in these sacred texts are spoken acts — they establish identity, destiny, and covenant. To accept a name is to enter into agreement with the meaning and authority behind it. To reject a name is to refuse that spiritual contract.

Likewise, to accept a curse name is to sign a contract with a lie.

Historical Labels as Spiritual Curses

The labels imposed during slavery and colonialism were not merely bureaucratic. They were spoken curses, often backed by law, religion, and violence. Each word — Negroid, Negro, the slur, and its colloquial offspring — functioned as a spiritual pronouncement:

- Negroid classified people as specimens.
- Negro erased tribal, national, and covenant identity.
- The slur branded inferiority onto the soul, reinforced by violence and mockery.
- The casual use of the colloquial form normalized the curse, turning external oppression into internal repetition.

These names were repeated in legal codes, sermons, songs, and everyday speech until they became invisible spiritual architecture — like ancient curses spoken over a bloodline, silently shaping generations.

Sermonic Break: A Prophetic Reminder

Who told you that was your name?

Who whispered it into your ears until you started answering to it?

Who labeled your lineage and then convinced you to wear it like a badge?

It wasn't God.

It wasn't your ancestors before captivity.

It was the curse.

And beloved, don't call yourself what the curse has called you.

Divine Renaming as Deliverance

Throughout the Torah, Bible, and Qur'an, God demonstrates His power to break curses through renaming:

- Abram → Abraham (Genesis 17): From exalted father to father of many nations — a new covenant destiny.
- Jacob → Israel (Genesis 32:28): From deceiver to "one who wrestles with God and prevails." His name change came after a night of wrestling — a spiritual struggle that

mirrors our own wrestling against inherited labels.

- Simon → Peter (Matthew 16:18): From instability to the rock of the church.
- Yahya (Surah Maryam 19:7): A divinely bestowed name marking a prophetic mission.

Renaming is not cosmetic; it's transformative. It severs old agreements and forges new ones. It declares to heaven, earth, and hell alike: This one's destiny has shifted.

The same spiritual principle applies to peoples and nations. When God calls a people by a new name, He is undoing what principalities tried to impose.

Wrestling with Principalities

Paul's revelation in Ephesians 6:12 pulls back the curtain:

"For we wrestle not against flesh and blood, but against principalities, against powers, against the rulers of the darkness of this world, against spiritual wickedness in high places."

This is not poetic language. It is strategic intelligence. Paul identifies that there are invisible hierarchies of evil—organized spiritual forces that operate through structures, systems, languages, and imaginations.

These forces:

- Inspire human systems to label and categorize.
- Animate ideologies that demean divine image-bearers.
- Whisper names that God did not speak.
- Establish linguistic strongholds to shape how a people sees themselves.

The labels forced upon Africans and their descendants—Negroid, Negro, the slur and its variants—were instruments through which these principalities erected strongholds. The goal was not only to control bodies but to colonize consciousness.

When people start answering to the curse, the enemy doesn't need chains—because the prison is in the mouth and mind.

Names as Spiritual Warfare

In the Torah, when Balak hired Balaam to curse Israel (Numbers 22–24), Balaam said plainly:

"How shall I curse whom God hath not cursed? or how shall I defy whom the LORD hath not defied?" (Numbers 23:8)

Balaam understood that curses operate through words. A people blessed by God cannot be cursed unless they agree with the curse. This principle runs like a thread through Scripture: agreement activates authority.

In the Qur'an, Allah warns believers:

"And do not pursue that of which you have no knowledge. Indeed, the hearing, the sight and the heart—about all those [one] will be questioned." — Surah Al-Isra 17:36

Accepting labels without questioning their origin is spiritually dangerous. It's a quiet form of surrender.

When an entire community adopts a name birthed in mockery, classification, or hatred—and repeats it among themselves as casual speech—they are not just using slang. They are unknowingly renewing spiritual contracts their ancestors never signed.

Renunciation and Reclamation

The pathway to freedom runs through awareness, renunciation, and reclamation.

1. Awareness

   Acknowledge that these labels were never neutral. They were crafted, imposed, and reinforced as spiritual and psychological weapons.

2. Renunciation

   Verbally and spiritually reject the false names. In biblical terms, this is breaking covenant with lies. In Qur'anic terms, it is turning away from mockery and falsehood (Surah Al-Hujurat 49:11). In Torah terms, it is refusing Balaam's curse.

3. Reclamation

   Receive and speak the name God gives—both individually and collectively. As God renamed Abram, Jacob, and Simon, so must a people reclaim their divine identity. This involves embracing ancestral names, divine descriptors, and new prophetic identities aligned with God's truth.

Prophetic Interlude

It is time to shut the mouth of the curse.

It is time to silence the echoes of principalities.

It is time to stop repeating what hell has whispered.

Child of God, people of promise: Don't call yourself what the curse has called you.

The Spiritual Weight of Words

"The LORD bless thee, and keep thee:

The LORD make his face shine upon thee, and be gracious unto thee:

The LORD lift up his countenance upon thee, and give thee peace.

And they shall put my name upon the children of Israel, and I will bless them." — Numbers 6:24-27

This priestly blessing demonstrates the divine logic: when God's name is placed upon a people, blessing flows. Conversely, when a cursed name is accepted, it opens the door for affliction.

Words are not neutral—they are spiritual vehicles. To carry a name is to carry the spiritual atmosphere attached to it.

A Final Exhortation

Beloved, the question still rings across the ages:

"Who told you that was your name?"

Was it God, who made you in His image?

Or was it the curse, spoken by systems and spirits bent on your erasure?

If it was the curse, then it is time—now—to reject it, renounce it, and reclaim the name Heaven has spoken over you.

Lift your head. Straighten your back. Let your tongue become the sword of the Spirit. Speak life. Speak truth. Speak destiny.

Don't call yourself what the curse has called you.

Not Who We Are

Part 2

THE RELEASE

Not Who We Are

Chapter 6
Linguistic Repentance: Renouncing the Curse

"Death and life are in the power of the tongue: and they that love it shall eat the fruit thereof."
— Proverbs 18:21

"The tongue also is a fire, a world of iniquity... it defileth the whole body, and setteth on fire the course of nature; and it is set on fire of hell."
— James 3:6

"Do you not see how Allah sets forth a parable: A good word is like a good tree—its root is firm and its branches reach the sky; it yields its fruit in every season by permission of its Lord. And the parable of a bad word is that of a bad tree, uprooted from the surface of the earth, having no stability."
— Qur'an 14:24-26

"And they shall put My name upon the children of Israel, and I will bless them."
— Numbers 6:27

The Tongue as the Battlefield

The war over identity ultimately comes down to the tongue. Empires can legislate, scholars can classify, and cultures can reinforce, but until a people's tongues agree, a curse remains external. The moment we begin to repeat the curse, it crosses the threshold from outside oppression to internal agreement.

33

Proverbs declares that death and life reside in the tongue. James calls it a fire that can set the entire course of life ablaze. The Qur'an likens words to trees, either deeply rooted in truth or easily uprooted lies. And the Torah shows us that when God's Name is spoken over a people, it activates blessing.

Words are not simply sounds — they are spiritual contracts. Each time we accept, repeat, or internalize a cursed name, we are in effect signing a covenant with it. But, blessed be God, covenants made by words can be broken by words. This is the heart of linguistic repentance.

What Is Linguistic Repentance?

Linguistic repentance is the conscious, verbal, and spiritual act of:

1. Recognizing the cursed words and names that have been spoken over you or your people.
1. Renouncing those words, breaking agreement with their origin and spiritual power.
1. Replacing them with God-given names, identities, and blessings.

It is repentance not for wrongdoing in the moral sense, but for participation in destructive language—often inherited unconsciously. It is a return to truth.

This practice has biblical, Torah, and Qur'anic precedent. In the Torah, when Jacob's name was changed to Israel (Genesis 32:28), he did not simply receive a new identity; he ceased to answer to the old one. In the Gospels, Simon became Peter when he confessed Jesus as the Christ (Matthew 16:18), marking a verbal and spiritual turning point. In the Qur'an, Allah directly bestows names like Yahya (John), declaring new identities as signs of His will (Surah Maryam 19:7).

Linguistic repentance follows this same divine pattern: turn away from the false name, embrace the true one.

The Spiritual Dynamics of Speech

There is a progression in how curses operate through language:

1. Silence — When a people are labeled and do not contest the label, silence functions as passive consent.

2. Repetition — When they begin to repeat the label, it embeds itself in their linguistic habits.

3. Confession — When they accept and confess the cursed identity as their own, it gains spiritual legal standing.

Conversely, freedom follows a reverse pattern:

1. Recognition — "This word is not mine."

2. Renunciation — "I break agreement with this word."

3. Replacement — "I receive and declare the name God has spoken."

This is why Paul writes in Romans 10:10, "For with the heart man believeth unto righteousness; and with the mouth confession is made unto salvation." Likewise, the Qur'an emphasizes the unity of belief and utterance (Surah Al-Baqarah 2:285), and the Torah repeatedly depicts covenantal blessings as spoken by priests and prophets (Numbers 6).

The tongue is not merely expressive; it is creative and legislative.

Steps of Linguistic Repentance

1. Recognition

The first step is to name the curse for what it is. Throughout this book we've examined how labels like Negroid, Negro, the slur, and its colloquial variants were engineered as linguistic weapons — and how they were spoken, sung, written, and reinforced until they became invisible scaffolding for identity.

Recognition means pulling these words out of invisibility. It's saying:

"This name does not come from God.

This label was never meant to define me.

This is not my inheritance."

In Torah terms, it's like Israel recognizing the foreign gods and tearing down their altars (Deuteronomy 12:3). In the New Testament, it echoes Jesus asking, "Who do you say that I am?" (Matthew 16:15), forcing a conscious confession. And in the Qur'an, it mirrors the call to discern truth from falsehood and follow the straight path (Surah Al-Fatiha).

2. Renunciation

Renunciation is verbal rejection. It is standing before God, your community, and the powers that be, and declaring:

"I break agreement with this cursed name.

I reject its power over my identity.

I sever the covenant it tried to make with me."

This is not emotional venting; it's spiritual legal language. It's like a witness revoking a forged signature.

- In Numbers 23, Balaam cannot curse whom God has blessed. When we renounce cursed names, we are stepping out from under unauthorized speech.
- In James 4:7, believers are told to "resist the devil, and he will flee from you." Resistance is not silence— it's speech that contradicts the lie.
- The Qur'an warns against mockery and name-calling (Surah Al-Hujurat 49:11), and calls the faithful to turn away from evil words, not accommodate them.

Renunciation breaks spiritual contracts forged by repetition and agreement.

3. Replacement

Finally, repentance is incomplete without replacement. Jesus didn't just cast out evil spirits; He filled the space with truth. God didn't just rename Abram; He gave him a new prophetic destiny.

Replacement involves embracing God-given identity—whether through ancestral names, divine titles (e.g., "chosen generation," "royal priesthood," 1 Peter 2:9), or personal prophetic affirmations.

In the Torah, God instructs priests to place His Name upon the people (Numbers 6:27). In the Qur'an, Allah bestows names that are unique and purposeful (Surah Maryam 19:7). This is the spiritual equivalent of changing the locks after evicting an intruder.

Prayers and Declarations

Personal Prayer of Renunciation

"Heavenly Father,

I come before You, acknowledging that words have power — life and death are in the tongue. I recognize that cursed names and labels have been spoken over my ancestors and over me. Today, I expose these words for what they are: spiritual curses, not divine names. I renounce every label that did not come from You. I break agreement with words that demean, dehumanize, and distort. I cancel every spiritual contract forged by repetition, silence, or acceptance. I receive the name You have spoken over me: chosen, beloved, holy, royal. Place Your Name upon me, as You did upon Israel, and bless me. Let my tongue speak life and truth from this day forward. In the authority of Your Word, I seal this renunciation. Amen."

Corporate Declaration

Leader: Who told you that was your name?

People: Not God. Not Truth.

Leader: Do you accept the curse?

People: We reject it.

Leader: Do you renounce the words that were spoken in hate, repeated in ignorance, and accepted in pain?

People: We renounce them now.

Leader: What name will you answer to?

People: The name God has given us — blessed, chosen, royal, holy.

Leader: What will you not do?

People: We will not call ourselves what the curse has called us!

Community Practice: Rewriting the Language of a People

While linguistic repentance begins in the heart and mouth of the individual, its greatest power is realized when entire families, congregations, communities, and generations embrace it. For centuries, cursed labels were reinforced not just through oppressors, but through communal repetition—songs, jokes, nicknames, and everyday language.

To break these patterns, communities can intentionally build new linguistic liturgies—ways of speaking that reinforce divine identity rather than inherited lies.

Here are a few practical frameworks:

1. Renunciation Ceremonies

Faith communities can hold public renunciation services, where individuals and families verbally reject cursed labels and affirm their God-given identities. This can be modeled after baptismal confessions or covenant renewal ceremonies. Scripture, Torah, and Qur'an passages can be read aloud, followed by communal declarations and blessings.

"And they shall put my name upon the children of Israel, and I will bless them." — Numbers 6:27

2. Name Sabbaths or Identity Days

Designate a day each year where the community focuses on teaching, remembering, and proclaiming divine names and ancestral identities. This can include workshops on name origins, cultural history, and prophetic identity declarations. Youth and elders alike can participate in speaking affirmations over one another.

3. Language Fasts

Challenge the community to abstain from using derogatory words and internalized slurs for a set period (e.g., 40 days). Instead, encourage intentional use of edifying language—God's words, Scriptural titles, and affirming cultural names. This fast trains the tongue to align with blessing, not bondage.

"A good word is like a good tree—its root is firm and its branches reach the sky." — Qur'an 14:24

4. Youth Empowerment Programs

Stereotypes and slurs often persist most strongly among the youth, where peer culture normalizes them. Empowering young people through education, history, spoken word, and declarations can transform the next generation into language reformers, not language imitators. When young voices stop echoing the curse, the chain weakens dramatically.

Closing Exhortation: Freedom on the Tongue

Beloved, linguistic repentance is not a performance — it is spiritual surgery. Every cursed word that once wrapped itself around your identity can be cut away by the sword of your own tongue, wielded in truth.

The Torah, the Bible, and the Qur'an all agree: words shape destiny, for blessing or for cursing. If words brought our people into linguistic bondage, words will lead us out.

This is not shame. This is freedom.

This is the act of a people waking up from linguistic amnesia, looking the curse in the eye, and saying,

"No more. I will not call myself what the curse has called me."

Chapter 7
Reclaiming the Divine Name

"Neither shall thy name any more be called Abram, but thy name shall be Abraham; for a father of many nations have I made thee."
— Genesis 17:5

"Thy name shall be called no more Jacob, but Israel: for as a prince hast thou power with God and with men, and hast prevailed."
— Genesis 32:28

"And I say also unto thee, That thou art Peter, and upon this rock I will build my church; and the gates of hell shall not prevail against it."
— Matthew 16:18

"'O Zachariah, indeed We give you good tidings of a boy whose name will be Yahya. We have not assigned to any before [this] name.'"
— Qur'an 19:7

The Power of a God-Given Name

When God renames, He does not merely alter a pronunciation; He rewrites destiny. Abram's transformation into Abraham marked the establishment of a covenant that would ripple through nations. Jacob's night of wrestling ended with a new identity—Israel—that would define a people for millennia. Simon's confession unlocked his transformation into Peter, the rock. In the Qur'an, Yahya (John) receives a divinely appointed name unlike any before him, signifying his unique prophetic role.

Across the Torah, the Bible, and the Qur'an, we see a consistent pattern:

41

When God speaks a name, He calls forth identity, destiny, and purpose.

The spiritual realm responds to names. Heaven recognizes divine names; hell respects covenant names; the earth aligns itself to prophetic declarations. This is why reclaiming the divine name is not vanity—it's an act of spiritual alignment.

Identity Restoration Through Renaming

The act of renaming in sacred texts always follows a divine encounter. It is never superficial.

- Abraham: His new name was the sign of God's covenant to make him the father of many nations (Genesis 17). The syllables carried promise.
- Israel: Jacob's identity changed at the point of struggle. His old name meant "supplanter" or "deceiver," but Israel means "one who wrestles with God and prevails" (Genesis 32:28). The name turned a personal history into a national destiny.
- Peter: Simon's identity shifted from instability to a foundation stone (Matthew 16:18).
- Yahya: Allah gave him a name unlike any before him (Qur'an 19:7), marking his prophetic uniqueness.

Each of these transformations demonstrates a universal spiritual principle: To walk in a new destiny, one must walk under a new name.

And the inverse is equally true: to remain under a cursed or false name is to remain tethered to a destiny that is not yours.

The Return to Ancestral and Prophetic Identity

For centuries, colonial labels overwrote ancestral names, tribal identities, and prophetic designations. People who once carried the names of nations, lineages, and covenants were reduced to racial taxonomies and slurs. To reclaim the divine name means to return to that which was overwritten—to lift the spiritual tarp off buried identity.

This involves two intertwined movements:

1. Reclaiming Cultural Names

Long before racial categories, there were tribes, clans, families, and prophetic destinies. Yoruba, Akan, Wolof, Igbo, Mandé, and countless others carried names imbued with meaning, prayer, and ancestral memory. Reclaiming these names is not nostalgia; it's identity warfare—reversing centuries of linguistic erasure.

"O mankind! Indeed We have created you from male and female and made you peoples and tribes that you may know one another. Indeed, the most noble of you in the sight of Allah is the most righteous of you. Indeed, Allah is Knowing and Acquainted." — Qur'an 49:13

God made tribes and peoples to know one another, not to be dissolved into foreign labels. Cultural names hold the memory of nations and the residue of prayers.

2. Embracing Prophetic and Scriptural Titles

Alongside ancestral names, believers must embrace the titles God has spoken over His people:

- "A chosen generation, a royal priesthood, a holy nation, His own special people." — 1 Peter 2:9
- "And they shall put My name upon the children of Israel, and I will bless them." — Numbers 6:27

These are not poetic flourishes; they are identity decrees. When communities repeatedly speak these divine titles over themselves, they are participating in God's renaming work.

The Role of Blessing in Naming

Blessing and naming are inseparable in the biblical, Torah, and Qur'anic worldview. To bless is often to name, and to name rightly is to bless.

In Numbers 6:22–27, the LORD commands Moses to teach Aaron and his sons how to bless the children of Israel:

"The LORD bless thee, and keep thee:

The LORD make his face shine upon thee, and be gracious unto thee:

The LORD lift up his countenance upon thee, and give thee peace.

And they shall put my name upon the children of Israel, and I will bless them."

Notice: the act of blessing is explicitly described as placing God's Name upon the people. That is how the blessing takes effect — the divine Name itself becomes the covering, the identity, the marker of favor.

In John 1:42, when Jesus meets Simon, He says:

"Thou art Simon the son of Jona: thou shalt be called Cephas" (which is by interpretation, a stone).

The blessing is embedded in the new name. Simon receives an identity that speaks of stability and purpose. From then on, even hell itself recognizes him by that name; his role in the Kingdom is tied to it.

In the Qur'an, Allah assigns Yahya's name before his birth:

"'O Zachariah, indeed We give you good tidings of a boy whose name will be Yahya. We have not assigned to any before [this] name.'" — Surah Maryam 19:7

Here, the divine act of naming precedes destiny. The name is not descriptive; it is prescriptive—defining the mission before the man is born.

This pattern is consistent: true identity flows from divine naming, and blessing flows from identity. Conversely, cursed naming blocks blessing by binding people to false destinies.

Practical Pathways to Reclaiming the Divine Name

The work of renaming is not merely theological; it is practical, communal, and generational. Here are pathways through which individuals and communities can actively rec laim divine naming:

1. Personal Practice

- Prayer and Journaling: Reflect on the names, labels, and titles you've accepted. Identify those that were spoken by God, those that came from your ancestors, and those that came from systems of oppression.
- Prophetic Declarations: Daily speak God's Word over yourself: "I am chosen. I am beloved. I am called by His Name." This is not vanity—it is spiritual alignment.
- Identity Encounters: Like Jacob wrestling with God, personal encounters through prayer, fasting, and reflection can reveal new names and purposes.

2. Family and Community Practice

- Naming Ceremonies: Restore the practice of intentional naming. Whether for newborns, teens, or adults reclaiming ancestral names, communities can gather to speak identity and blessing over individuals.
- Rites of Passage: Many cultures historically marked identity transitions through naming. Reviving these rituals embeds divine identity deeply in community memory.

- Elders' Blessings: In both biblical and African traditions, elders speak blessings over the young. Imagine elders standing over a new generation, declaring divine titles, ancestral honor, and prophetic destiny.

3. Public and Cultural Practice

- Media, Music, and Art: Names are reinforced through what communities sing, display, and celebrate. Reclaiming identity requires cultural production that glorifies divine naming rather than echoing curses.
- Educational Curricula: Teaching children their ancestral histories and scriptural identities inoculates them against foreign labels.
- Public Declarations: Churches, mosques, schools, and community centers can hold Identity Proclamation Days, where people declare their divine and ancestral names publicly.

"Say: My prayer and my sacrifice and my life and my death are for Allah, the Lord of the worlds." — Qur'an 6:162

This verse captures the essence of identity alignment: the entire life is oriented around divine reality, including speech and naming.

Chapter 8
A Global Call to Action

"The LORD gave the word: great was the company of those that published it."
— Psalm 68:11

"And let us not be weary in well doing: for in due season we shall reap, if we faint not."
— Galatians 6:9

"Indeed, Allah will not change the condition of a people until they change what is in themselves."
— Qur'an 13:11

A New Sound Rising

History has witnessed moments when a single shift in language set entire nations in motion. Words have always carried more than syllables—they carry spirit, identity, and power.

We have traced how labels forged in spiritual wickedness and colonial design became instruments of bondage. We have walked the path from recognition to renunciation, from linguistic repentance to divine reclamation.

But this journey cannot end in private revelation. What began as personal awakening must now become public movement. A new sound must rise—not from pulpits alone, but from classrooms, boardrooms, studios, and family tables.

This is a call to nations, tribes, tongues, and communities to collectively reject cursed labels and to speak life into generations yet unborn.

The Power of Collective Language Shifts

Throughout history, when people changed how they spoke, they changed how they lived:

- The Abolition Movement reframed enslaved Africans not as property but as men and women created in God's image.
- The Civil Rights Movement declared, "I AM a Man," and the linguistic landscape of a nation began to shift.
- Post-colonial movements across Africa and Asia reclaimed indigenous names of countries, cities, and peoples— Léopoldville became Kinshasa, Gold Coast became Ghana, Southern Rhodesia became Zimbabwe.

Language has always been the first territory of liberation. Once a people name themselves rightly, they govern themselves differently.

"And all the people gathered themselves together as one man into the street that was before the water gate; and they spake unto Ezra the scribe to bring the book of the law of Moses, which the LORD had commanded to Israel." — Nehemiah 8:1

In Nehemiah's time, national restoration began with the public reading of the Word, aligning communal language with divine covenant.

Similarly, in the Qur'an, Surah Al-Tawbah records entire communities turning collectively in repentance and realignment with Allah's command. Communal linguistic repentance precedes societal transformation.

Mobilizing Faith Communities

Faith communities are uniquely positioned to lead this linguistic revolution. Churches, mosques, synagogues, and temples are centers of speech—where words shape worldviews, prayers frame reality, and songs carry theology into the soul.

1. **Teaching and Preaching:**

   Ministers, imams, rabbis, and teachers must teach the origins, connotations, and spiritual power of language. Sermons, khutbahs, and studies should confront the history of cursed labels and unveil God's pattern of naming.

2. **Ritual Renunciation:**

   In the same way that communities practice baptism, shahada, circumcision, or bar/bat mitzvahs as covenantal rites, so too can communities hold linguistic renunciation ceremonies—publicly breaking agreement with false names and declaring divine identities.

3. **Prophetic Naming:**

   Faith leaders can speak new names over individuals and communities, as Jesus did with Simon, as God did with Abram and Jacob, as Allah did with Yahya. When spiritual authorities speak truth, heaven echoes, and earth responds.

   "Then those who feared the LORD spoke with one another. The LORD paid attention and heard them, and a book of remembrance was written before him of those who feared the LORD and esteemed his name." — Malachi 3:16

Communities that esteem the divine Name and refuse cursed language become centers of linguistic light in a darkened world.

Engaging Cultural Institutions

Faith communities may lead, but cultural institutions amplify. The words that shape generations are often sung in songs, spoken in classrooms, printed in headlines, or streamed through digital platforms.

To shift language globally, we must engage media, education, and the arts not merely as spectators, but as strategic architects of cultural speech.

1. Education

Schools are linguistic incubators. For centuries, colonial education systems reinforced racial hierarchies through textbooks, euphemisms, and omission. A global call to action must involve rewriting curricula to:

- Teach the true history and etymology of racial labels.
- Celebrate ancestral languages, tribal identities, and divine titles.
- Train students to discern language critically and spiritually.

Just as Moses instructed Israel to "teach these words diligently to your children" (Deuteronomy 6:7), so too must communities ensure that linguistic truth is taught intentionally, not assumed passively.

2. Media

Words shape imagination, and media shapes words. Faith-based media, community newspapers, digital platforms, and entertainment industries must make editorial and creative choices that align with truth. This includes:

- Refusing to normalize slurs and cursed labels, even "colloquially."
- Elevating programming that tells stories of ancestral identity and divine calling.
- Creating documentaries, podcasts, music, and literature that reclaim language.

"Say: My prayer and my sacrifice and my life and my death are for Allah, the Lord of the worlds." — Qur'an 6:162

Every medium must become an altar upon which words are offered intentionally, not casually.

3. Arts and Culture

Throughout history, the arts have preserved memory. From griots and poets to playwrights and painters, artistic expression has been the archive of identity. When artists reclaim divine naming and ancestral language, they do more than create beauty—they heal cultural amnesia.

Imagine plays that retell the stories of Abram, Jacob, Simon, and Yahya as identity dramas. Imagine murals, music, and spoken word that dismantle curses and awaken destinies. This is not entertainment; this is cultural prophecy.

Raising a New Generation

The true test of any movement is whether it outlives its founders. If linguistic repentance ends with us, the curse can return through the mouths of the young. But if the next generation is trained as language reformers, the victory endures.

1. Youth Education and Mentorship

- Teach young people the history and power of names in Scripture, Torah, and Qur'an.
- Expose them early to ancestral languages, names, and titles.
- Equip them to challenge cursed language in their peer groups with wisdom and confidence.

2. Empowering Youth Voices

Give young poets, rappers, writers, and speakers platforms to create new linguistic culture. Let them lead in crafting chants, slogans, songs, and stories that celebrate divine identity.

3. Rites of Passage

Design spiritual and cultural rites that mark transitions in youth identity—naming ceremonies, blessing services, or "identity graduations." In these moments, elders speak blessing names over young people, just as Isaac spoke over Jacob, Jacob over his sons, and elders over prophets.

"Train up a child in the way he should go: and when he is old, he will not depart from it." — Proverbs 22:6

Youth are not merely recipients of this movement—they are its multipliers.

Engaging Cultural Institutions

Faith communities may lead, but cultural institutions amplify. The words that shape generations are often sung in songs, spoken in classrooms, printed in headlines, or streamed through digital platforms.

To shift language globally, we must engage media, education, and the arts not merely as spectators, but as strategic architects of cultural speech.

1. Education

Schools are linguistic incubators. For centuries, colonial education systems reinforced racial hierarchies through textbooks, euphemisms, and omission. A global call to action must involve rewriting curricula to:

- Teach the true history and etymology of racial labels.
- Celebrate ancestral languages, tribal identities, and divine titles.
- Train students to discern language critically and spiritually.

Just as Moses instructed Israel to "teach these words diligently to your children" (Deuteronomy 6:7), so too must communities ensure that linguistic truth is taught intentionally, not assumed passively.

2. Media

Words shape imagination, and media shapes words. Faith-based media, community newspapers, digital platforms, and entertainment industries must make editorial and creative choices that align with truth. This includes:

- Refusing to normalize slurs and cursed labels, even "colloquially."
- Elevating programming that tells stories of ancestral identity and divine calling.
- Creating documentaries, podcasts, music, and literature that reclaim language.

"Say: My prayer and my sacrifice and my life and my death are for Allah, the Lord of the worlds." — Qur'an 6:162

Every medium must become an altar upon which words are offered intentionally, not casually.

3. Arts and Culture

Throughout history, the arts have preserved memory. From griots and poets to playwrights and painters, artistic expression has been the archive of identity. When artists reclaim divine naming and ancestral language, they do more than create beauty—they heal cultural amnesia.

Imagine plays that retell the stories of Abram, Jacob, Simon, and Yahya as identity dramas. Imagine murals, music, and spoken word that dismantle curses and awaken destinies. This is not entertainment; this is cultural prophecy.

Raising a New Generation

The true test of any movement is whether it outlives its founders. If linguistic repentance ends with us, the curse can return through the mouths of the young. But if the next generation is trained as language reformers, the victory endures.

1. Youth Education and Mentorship

- Teach young people the history and power of names in Scripture, Torah, and Qur'an.
- Expose them early to ancestral languages, names, and titles.
- Equip them to challenge cursed language in their peer groups with wisdom and confidence.

2. Empowering Youth Voices

Give young poets, rappers, writers, and speakers platforms to create new linguistic culture. Let them lead in crafting chants, slogans, songs, and stories that celebrate divine identity.

3. Rites of Passage

Design spiritual and cultural rites that mark transitions in youth identity—naming ceremonies, blessing services, or "identity graduations." In these moments, elders speak blessing names over young people, just as Isaac spoke over Jacob, Jacob over his sons, and elders over prophets.

"Train up a child in the way he should go: and when he is old, he will not depart from it." — Proverbs 22:6

Youth are not merely recipients of this movement—they are its multipliers.

A Prophetic Global Declaration

Every movement that has changed the world has ended with a declaration—a shared articulation of values and vision that transcends borders and generations. Just as Moses declared the covenant to Israel, Nehemiah led national repentance, and Muhammad proclaimed the Oneness of God to tribes and nations, so too must we speak as one.

This is not merely a manifesto for one ethnic group; it is a universal spiritual strategy for any people who have been misnamed by history and misidentified by oppressive systems.

Wherever cursed labels have been normalized, this call to action applies.

The Global Linguistic Reclamation Manifesto

We, a people awakened to truth,

Recognize that words shape destinies.

We reject names spoken in hatred,

Forged in the fires of spiritual wickedness,

And repeated across generations as if they were our own.

We repent of every agreement we have made—knowingly or unknowingly—

With cursed language that diminished our God-given identity.

We renounce the old labels and reclaim the divine names

Spoken by our Creator, affirmed by our ancestors, and sealed in covenant.

We will teach our children their true names.

We will sing our songs with clarity.

We will shape curricula, media, and art that tell the truth.

We will bless rather than curse, build rather than mimic,

And declare identities rooted in heaven, not hell.

We call upon faith leaders, educators, artists, parents, and youth:

Take up this mantle. Reform your tongues. Reshape your speech.

Build communities where God's Name is honored and cursed names are banished.

We do this not in pride, but in obedience.

Not to glorify ourselves, but to glorify the One who named us before the foundations of the world.

We will not call ourselves what the curse has called us.

We will call ourselves what God has called us.

Closing Charge

"The LORD gave the word: great was the company of those that published it." — Psalm 68:11

This is your moment to become part of that company—those who publish a new word into the atmosphere of nations. Let pulpits, classrooms, studios, and dinner tables resound with names of truth. Let communities everywhere awaken to the realization that language is spiritual territory, and it must be governed righteously.

"And Allah presents an example: a good word is like a good tree, its root is firm and its branches reach to the sky." — Qur'an 14:24

"I have set before you life and death, blessing and cursing: therefore choose life, that both thou and thy seed may live." — Deuteronomy 30:19

This is the choice before us now: continue repeating what history's curses have spoken, or raise up a new generation under the canopy of God's spoken blessing.

Lift your voice.

Publish the word.

Teach the young.

Shape the culture.

And above all—

Don't call yourself what the curse has called you.
Call yourself what God has called you.

Discussion Questions

Reflect

1. What labels or names have been spoken over your life that did not come from God?
2. How has language—spoken by family, culture, or media—shaped your sense of identity?
3. When have you witnessed words being used as tools of either liberation or bondage?
4. Which biblical, Torah, or Qur'anic stories of renaming resonate most with your own experience?

Repent

5. What words or phrases have you personally repeated that you now recognize as spiritually destructive?
6. How can you begin practicing linguistic repentance—renouncing the false and embracing the true?
7. In what ways can communities publicly reject cursed language and replace it with blessing?

Reclaim

8. What does it mean to you to "put on" a divine or ancestral name?
9. How can your faith community, classroom, or family reinforce God-given identities in everyday speech?
10. What new language, song, or declaration could you create that reflects who you truly are?

Appendix A: Study Questions & Reflections

For the Preface

1. When you think back over your own life, what was the first time you realized that language could wound—or heal?

2. Why do you think God allows human beings to possess the creative power of speech?

3. How does your family's or community's use of language shape your sense of worth or destiny today?

Chapter 1 – The Tongue as a Weapon and a Wand

1. What scriptures teach us that words carry both creative and destructive power?

2. How does understanding speech as spiritual technology change the way you listen and speak?

3. Have you ever spoken something over yourself—or allowed others to—that later felt like a curse? How can you replace it with a blessing?

4. Write a personal declaration that uses the Word of God to speak life over your future.

Chapter 2 – The Five Words That Bound a People

1. Which of the five words (Negroid, Negro, Niggard, Nigger, Nigga) do you see most active in modern culture?

2. How do you distinguish between cultural "reclamation" of a word and spiritual repetition of a curse?

3. Why is it vital for a community to understand the history of its own naming?

4. What new word or phrase could you introduce in your circle that speaks dignity, unity, and purpose?

Chapter 3 – The Curse Behind the Words

1. What evidence do you see that language has been used deliberately to control identity?

2. How does Ephesians 6:12—"We wrestle not against flesh and blood"—reframe how you see racism, colonialism, and identity politics?

3. Which spiritual disciplines (prayer, fasting, studying, confession) might help break internalized linguistic curses?

4. What would it look like to choose life in your speech this week?

Chapter 4 – Psychological Warfare: Stereotypes as Chains

1. How do stereotypes operate as invisible forms of psychological warfare?

2. What modern media examples continue to reinforce stereotypes that began centuries ago?

3. How does scripture challenge the idea that human value can be ranked by race, class, or culture?

4. In your own life, how can you consciously replace the old stereotype with a new story?

Chapter 5 – Who Told You That Was Your Name?

1. What does God's question to Adam—"Who told you that you were naked?"—reveal about false narratives?

2. Have you ever believed something about yourself that God never said? What caused that agreement?

3. What does it mean to "renounce" a false identity? How do you do that spiritually?

4. Write a new affirmation that declares who you are according to God's Word.

Chapter 6 – Linguistic Repentance: Renouncing the Curse

- What does repentance sound like in speech?
- How can confession become a linguistic cleansing of the soul?

Chapter 7 – Reclaiming the Divine Name

- What do the stories of Abram, Jacob, and Simon teach about divine renaming?
- How does a new name restore purpose and identity?

Chapter 8 – A Global Call to Action

- How can churches, mosques, and community groups work together to restore truth in language?
- What one action will you personally take to help your generation speak words of life?

Appendix B: Notes and References

Sacred Texts and Scripture

1. Torah / Hebrew Bible

   - Genesis 1 – Creation by the spoken Word.

   - Genesis 17 – Abram renamed Abraham; covenantal identity.

   - Genesis 32 – Jacob renamed Israel; struggle and blessing.

   - Numbers 6:22-27 – Priestly blessing and divine naming.

   - Deuteronomy 30:19 – Life and death set before humanity; choose life.

   - Psalm 83:4 – Erasure of a nation's name as spiritual warfare.

   - Proverbs 18:21 – Power of life and death in the tongue.

2. Bible (New Testament)

   - Matthew 16:18 – Simon renamed Peter.

   - James 3:5-8 – The tongue's destructive and creative power.

   - Ephesians 6:12 – Conflict with principalities and powers.

   - 2 Corinthians 10:5 – Casting down arguments and false exaltations.

3. Qur'an
- Surah Ibrahim 14:24-27 – The good word as a good tree.
- Surah Maryam 19:7 – Yahya named directly by Allah.
- Surah Al-Hujurat 49:11 – Prohibition against mocking and offensive nicknames.
- Surah Ar-Ra'd 13:11 – Allah changes not the condition of a people until they change what is in themselves.

Historical and Linguistic Sources

1. Blumenbach, Johann Friedrich. On the Natural Varieties of Mankind. 1775 / 1795.

2. Gould, Stephen Jay. The Mismeasure of Man. New York: W. W. Norton, 1981.

3. Fredrickson, George M. Racism: A Short History. Princeton University Press, 2002.

4. Winthrop Jordan, White Over Black: American Attitudes Toward the Negro, 1550-1812. 1968.

5. Oxford English Dictionary, entries for "Negro," "Niggard," and "Nigger."

6. Appiah, Kwame Anthony, and Henry Louis Gates Jr., eds. Africana: The Encyclopedia of the African and African-American Experience. 2005.

7. Du Bois, W.E.B. The Souls of Black Folk. 1903.

8. Fanon, Frantz. Black Skin, White Masks. 1952.

9. hooks, bell. Talking Back: Thinking Feminist, Thinking Black. 1989.

10. Cone, James H. Black Theology and Black Power. 1969.

Modern Psychology and Sociolinguistics

1. Steele, Claude M. "Race and the Fragility of the American Self." Atlantic Monthly, 1992.

2. Steele, Claude M. Whistling Vivaldi: How Stereotypes Affect Us and What We Can Do. W.W. Norton, 2010.

3. Freire, Paulo. Pedagogy of the Oppressed. Continuum, 1970.

4. Tatum, Beverly Daniel. Why Are All the Black Kids Sitting Together in the Cafeteria? 1997.

5. Ladson-Billings, Gloria. Critical Race Theory in Education. 2009.

Suggested Further Reading

- Moten, Fred. In the Break: The Aesthetics of the Black Radical Tradition.

- Davis, Angela Y. Women, Race & Class.

- Asante, Molefi Kete. The Afrocentric Idea.

- Anderson, Benedict. Imagined Communities.

- Baldwin, James. The Fire Next Time.

About the Author

Aaron Maxwell Montague is a pastor, veteran, life coach, and visionary author whose mission is to awaken divine identity in individuals and communities.

A retired member of the United States Navy, achieving the rate of First Class Petty Officer and designation of Master Training Specialist.

After military service, he assumed a new career with the premier Veterans Serving Organization in the United States. This work culminated after 24 years, Aaron retired as the National Appeals Officer Supervisor, of the nearly 1million member organization in Washington, D.C., advocating for the men and women who served their country.

Aaron is the founder of Montague Motivational Ministries (MX3) and the creator of the West Philadelphia Billionaires Society (WPBS)—a movement dedicated to building community-owned wealth, generational prosperity, and faith-driven leadership.

As a certified life coach, NLP practitioner, and trance therapist, his ministry and teaching blend spiritual insight with psychological wisdom, helping people renew their minds, rewrite their internal language, and rediscover their purpose in God.

A passionate Bible teacher and associate pastor at Kingdom Celebration Center, Aaron delivers messages that are both prophetic and practical—rooted in Scripture, infused with compassion, and charged with divine urgency.

He writes and speaks with the conviction that language shapes destiny and that we must never call ourselves what the curse has called us.

Aaron resides with his beloved wife, Wanda "God-Is-Love" Montague, whose kindness, wisdom, and strength inspire every word he writes.

His life and work proclaim one message:

We are not who they said we are.

We are who God says we are.

www.ingramcontent.com/pod-product-compliance
Lightning Source LLC
Chambersburg PA
CBHW051234120626
46547CB00013B/1637